The 'Mary Had a Little Lamb' Book

for Cello

by Cassia Harvey

CHP167
©2006 by C. Harvey Publications All Rights Reserved.
www.charveypublications.com - print books & free sheet music blog
www.learnstrings.com - PDF downloadable books & chamber music

1. Mary Had a Little Lamb

Hale, arr. Harvey

2. Mary Had Some Whole Notes

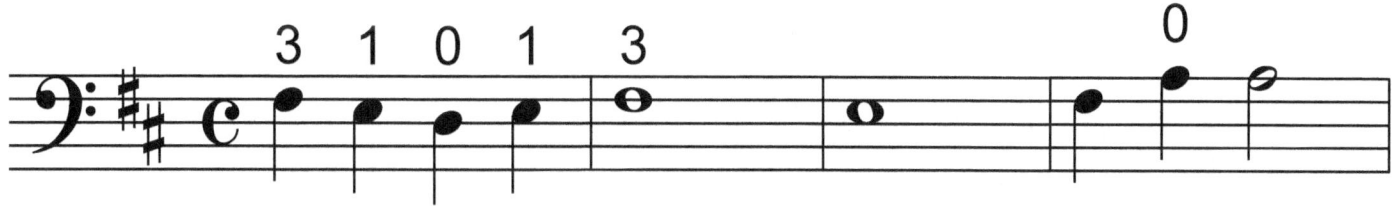

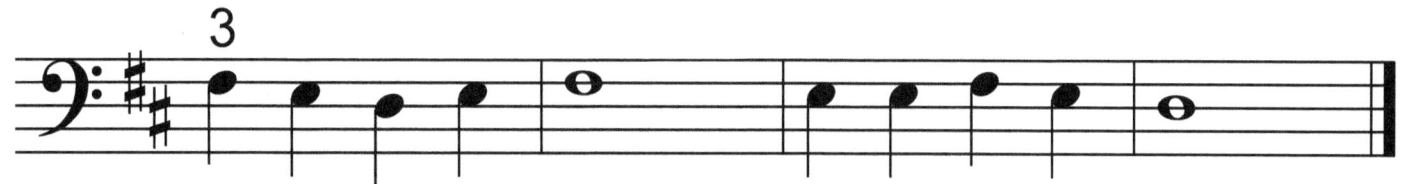

©2006 C. Harvey Publications All Rights Reserved.

3. Mary Runs After the Lamb

4. Mary's Rhythm

5. Lamb's Rhythm

©2006 C. Harvey Publications All Rights Reserved.

6. Crossing Strings to Find Her Lamb

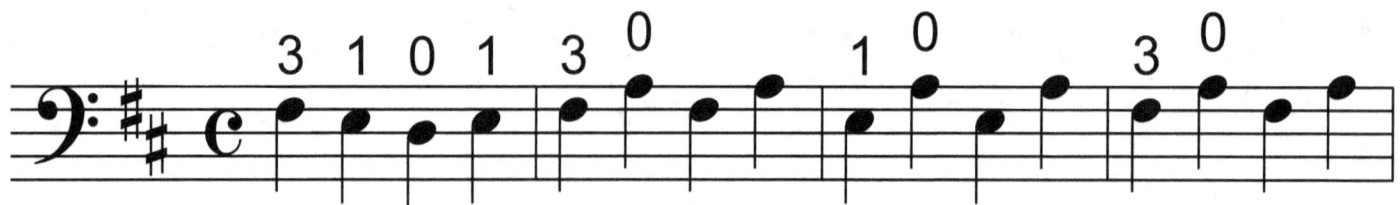

7. Running and Crossing Strings

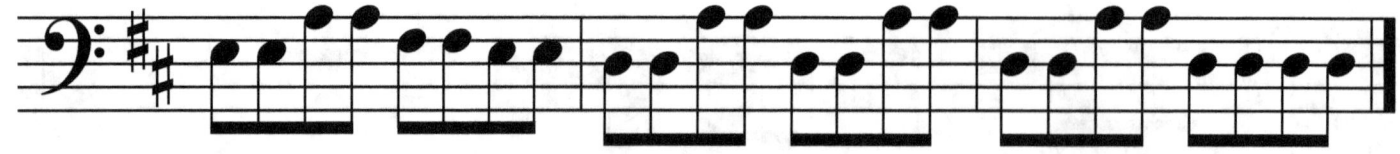

8. Mary is Marching

9. Playing Slurs with Mary

10. Mary Had a Little Lamb on G

11. Lamb Rhythm

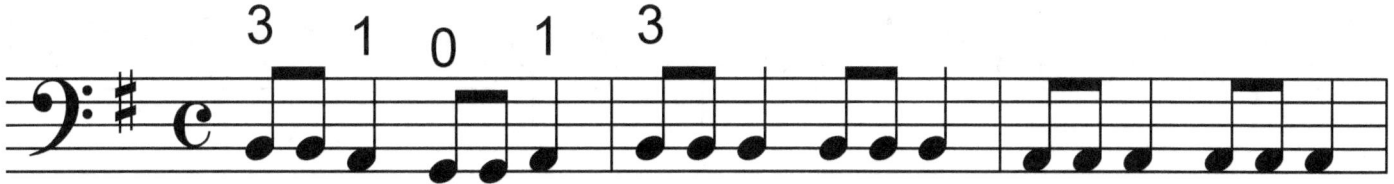

12. Mary's String Changing

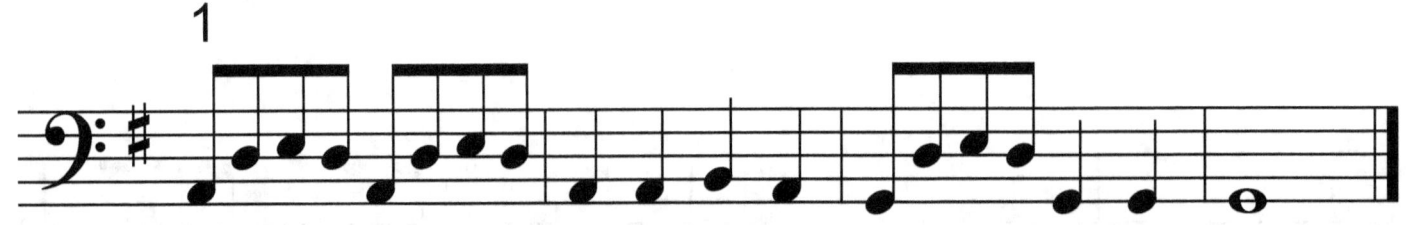

13. Mary's Finger Exercise

14. Mary Had a Little Lamb on C

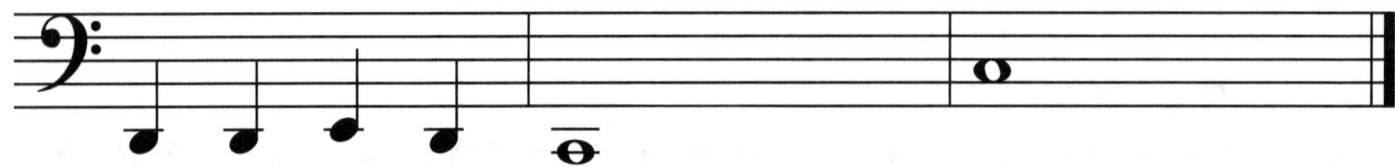

15. Lamb With Dotted Half Notes

16. Mary's Rhythm

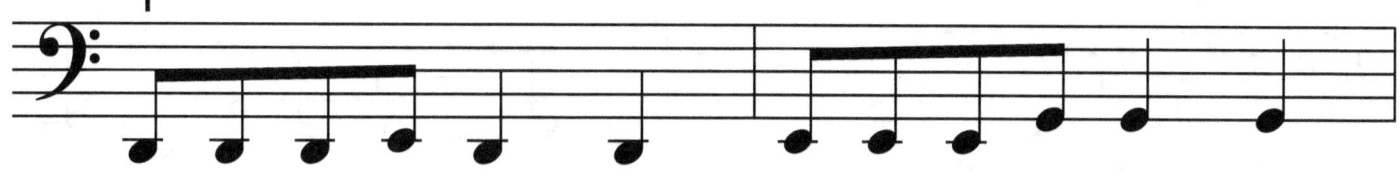
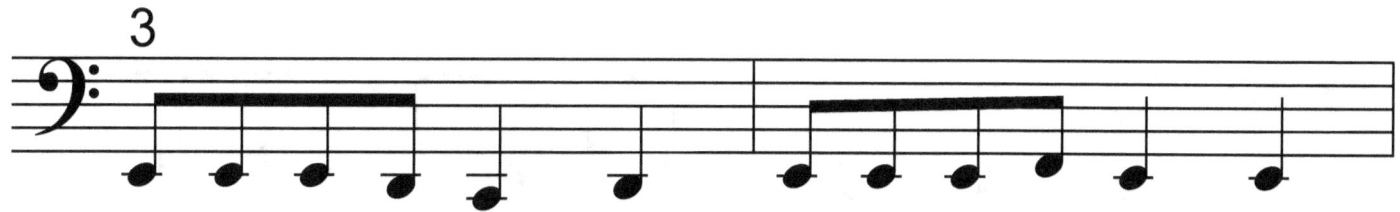

17. Mary Changes Strings

18. Mary Lost Her Little Lamb

19. Lost Lamb Slurs

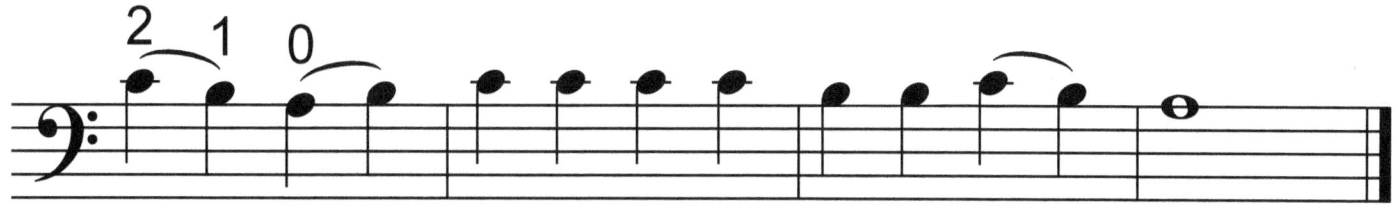

©2006 C. Harvey Publications All Rights Reserved.

20. Mary Lost Her Little Lamb on D

21. Lost Lamb in 3/4

22. Mary Lost Her Little Lamb on G

23. Lost Lamb in 6/8

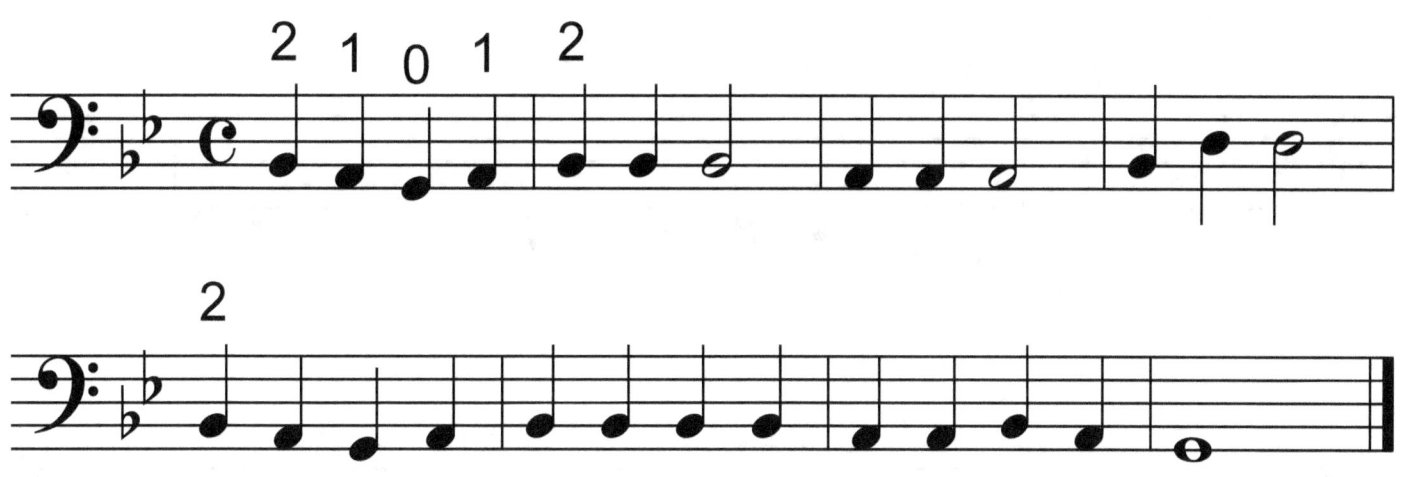

24. Mary Lost Her Little Lamb on C

25. Lost Lamb in 2/4

26. Mary Starts on First Finger

27. Lamb Slurs

28. Mary's 6/8 Counting

29. Lamb Stops

30. Mary Starts on First Finger

31. Mary's Rhythm

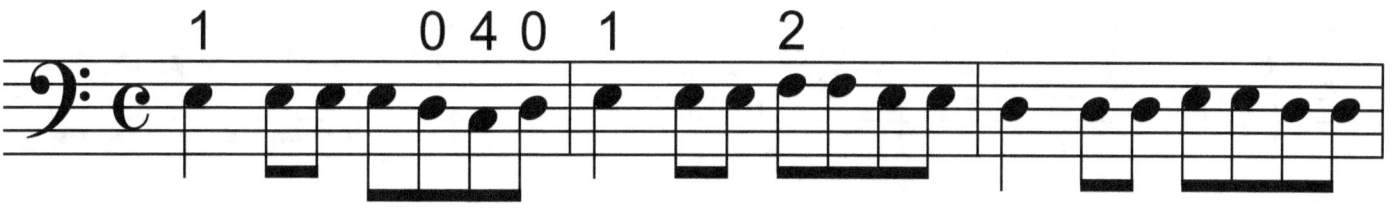

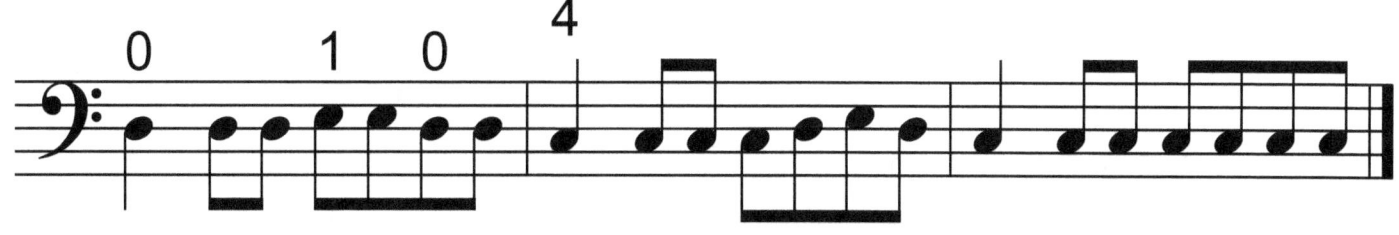

32. Lamb Slurs

33. Mary Starts on First Finger

34. Lamb Dance in 6/8

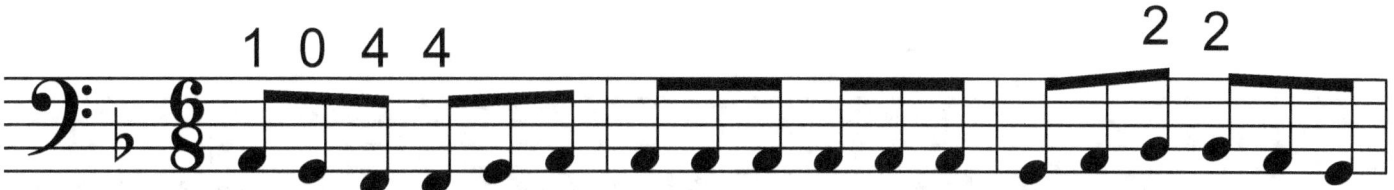

35. Mary's Slurs

36. Mary Goes Running

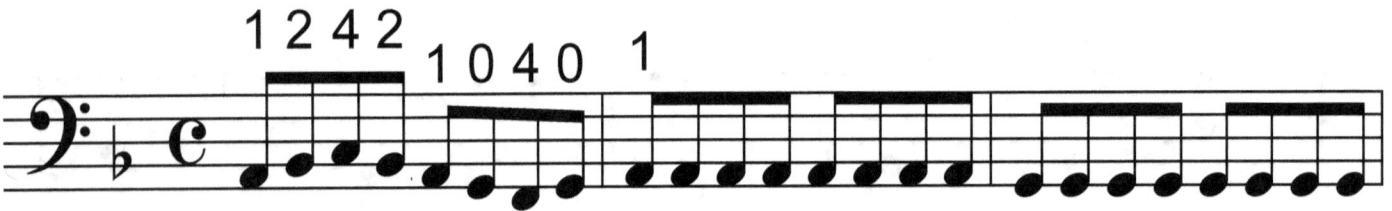

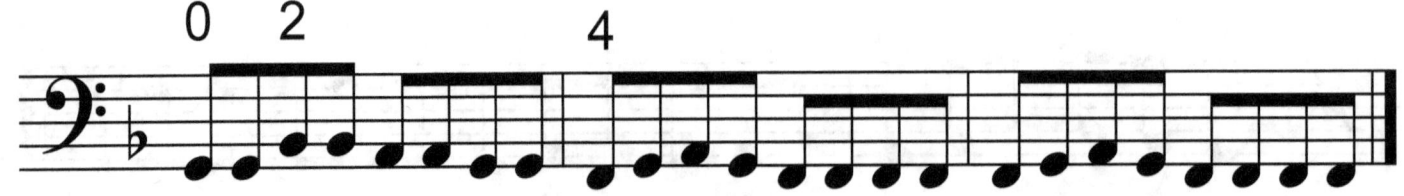

37. Mary Starts on Open A

38. Lamb Crossing

39. Mary's Rhythm

40. Mary Starts on Open D

41. Mary's Dotted Quarter Notes

42. Mary in 3/4

43. Lamb Stops

44. Mary Starts on Open G

45. Lamb in 3/4

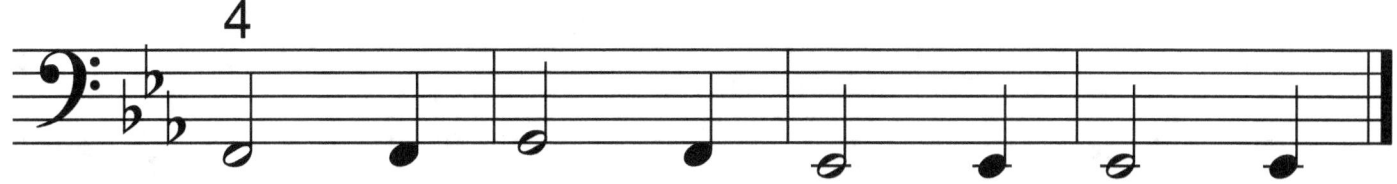

46. Mary Rests

47. Lamb Octaves

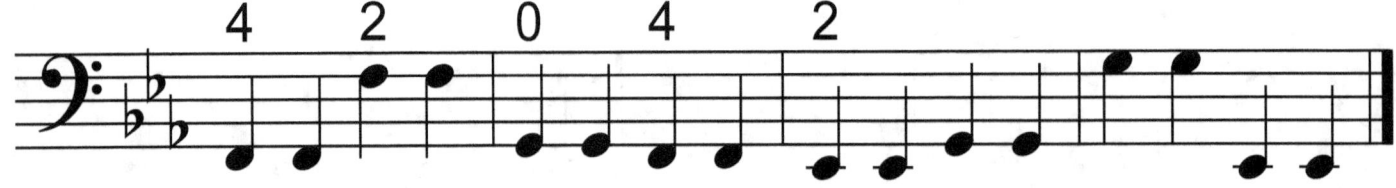

48. Lamb Bowing

49. Mary's Fiddle Tune

50. The Lamb's Fiddle Tune

available from **www.charveypublications.com**: CHP305

Beginning Fiddle Duets for Two Cellos

Cripple Creek

Trad., arr. Myanna Harvey

©2016 C. Harvey Publications All Rights Reserved.